This book is dedicated to busy people
with important things to say.

Eugene Moreau

Introduction	5
Inspiration	6

Headline One: Clarity

Five Question Foundation	9
Five Question Master Page	16
Developing A Speech Mindset	17

Headline Two: Content

Build Content Around A Theme	21
Identify Key Points	23
Support Key Points	24
Common Story Types	26
Five Essentials For Telling An Outstanding Story	27
Keeping The Attention Of Your Audience	31
Using Humor	33
Types Of Humor	34

Headline Three: The 13 Box Structure

The Five Steps Of Writing	41
Delivering A 13 Box Speech	51
13 Box Structure Chart Model	51
The Final Words	52
A Little About Me	53
What People Are Saying...	54

Introduction

Being the person who stands in front of an audience as a public speaker can be both invigorating and daunting. It is invigorating because you are overcoming one of the greatest fears that humans face and it is daunting for exactly that reason!

little book promises to deliver ools you need to become an anding public speaker.

This is a big claim!

Public speaking has been listed as the number one human fear by hundreds of surveys in many different countries. Number One! To put it in perspective, the fear of death is usually around number four.

This little black book can help bring that fear down your list - and change your life along the way, if you let it.

It might be some relief for you to know that great communicators are not born - they are made. You can be one of them. The ability to get your message across, clearly, confidently, and persuasively, is a skill that can be learned, practiced and perfected by anyone who makes the decision to be an outstanding public speaker.

It may take some people longer, and they may have to work harder than others, but the truth is if a person wants to achieve it, they can.

That is my promise to you. If you want to be a standout public speaker then this book will deliver the tools you need to be just that.

Eugene Moreau

eugene@moreaucommunications.com

Inspiration

I'd like to share with you one of my most memorable experiences from the other side of the lectern. After all these years there's nothing I like more than listening to a really good speaker.

The person I'm going to tell you about has stayed in my mind since the day I sat in that stadium and heard him speak.

His name is Og Mandino and I will never forget listening to him speak. During his life he wrote 17 books and gave talks to hundreds of thousands of people all over the world. He was the president of "Success Unlimited" until 1976, when at the age of 52, he devoted himself to full-time writing and lecturing.

Og Mandino was one of the most sought after speakers in the United States and was inducted as a member of the National Speakers Association Hall of Fame.

When I first heard him, he held me enthralled for more than an hour with his gentle, yet incredibly powerful words.

One minute his voice had the intensity of fire, then, within a few heartbeats, it was like soothing balm.

He stood behind a podium on a very large stage (the audience numbered around 8000) yet when he shifted just a few inches to his left, we followed the subtle movement, riveted by this elderly, soft spoken man.

It was then that I understood the difference between a really good communicator and someone who just stands in front of people and talks.

That experience inspired me to write this book. It is to help people like you and me...busy...focused...ambitious - become more powerful public speakers.

I encourage you to come back to this little book more than once and learn it's secrets. You can use these tools, principles and techniques every time you are asked to give a speech. they will not let you down.

Use it and one day I know, I'll be sitting in an audience again being riveted by a really professional speaker – **YOU!**

Headline One
CLARITY

Five Question Foundation

So you have been invited to give a speech.

Congratulations.

Now, let's work together to do justice to the invitation and help you become an outstanding public speaker. The first step is to gain a clear picture of 'motive'. By that I mean you will need to know the answers to five specific questions:

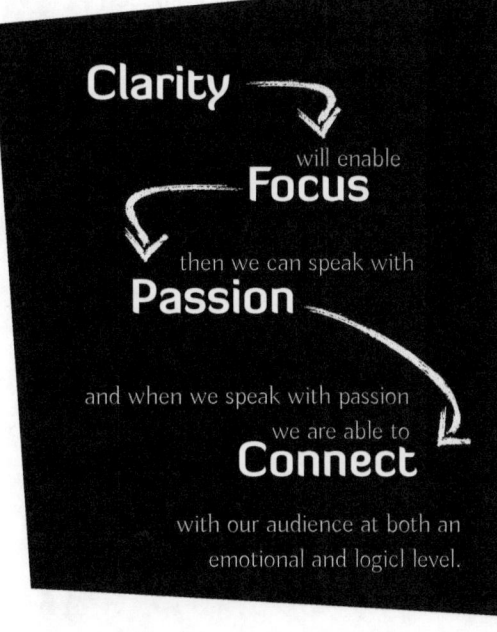

Clarity will enable Focus then we can speak with Passion and when we speak with passion we are able to Connect with our audience at both an emotional and logicl level.

1. Why was I asked to give this speech?

2. What is my topic and goal?

3. Who will I be speaking to?

4. Why will they listen to me?

5. How long do I have to speak?

Answering these five questions will enable you to move forward with great clarity and focus.

When you are able to gain clarity and have focus then you can speak with passion.

When you speak with passion you are able to connect with your audience at both an emotional and logical level.

Gaining clarity and focus goes beyond the basic 'tell them what your going to say, say it, and then tell them what you said' model. Let's face it. Most of us can think on our feet if we know what it is we are talking about.

Most of us can also establish a form of rapport and chemistry with people, especially if we know them or have met them before.

So, to build on this foundation most of us already have, we need to be able to answer these basic questions before we can even begin to work on our speech.

Question One
Why was I asked to give this speech?

This is an important question that needs to be answered before you can we even consider developing a theme or structure for your speech.

Can you imagine turning up with a well-rehearsed speech that informs and educates when your audience is celebrating a milestone and they are expecting you to be funny and entertaining?

Fronting up fully loaded for something challenging and logical when your audience is looking for a laugh would be a nightmare in anyone's books.

By knowing the reason you have been asked to speak, you are guaranteeing your speech will be appropriate for your audience.

There are usually four reasons why you will be asked to speak: to entertain, to persuade, to motivate or to educate.

1. Entertain
Create fun and energy with your audience through witty dialogue and very sharp lines.

2. Persuade
Convince your audience to accept a point of view that requires change or buying into.

3. Motivate
Enthuse your audience to do more of what they are already doing really well - only better.

4. Educate
Impart specific knowledge on a practical issue or nature to your audience.

These four reasons can be stand alone, or they can be joined in any combination.

Question Two
What is my topic and goal?

This question sets up your whole speech because it answers the driving question, 'What am I trying to accomplish?' It is best if you shape your answer to this question into a single sentence.

What am I setting out to **accomplish** with this speech?

For example, you could say: "I want the audience to **know** our company must make changes to avoid going out of business."

"I want the audience to **support** this initiative by volunteering or giving money."

"I want the audience to **vote** for adding a new art programme in our school."

"I want the audience to **understand** how our product or service can increase revenue opportunities."

Notice how the examples above are specific? They have identified both a topic and a goal to be achieved as a result of the speech.

You cannot hit a target you cannot see. You find the bulls-eye of your speech by writing what you want to happen in one single statement.

Question Three
Who will I be speaking to?

Now that you have a very clear picture of why and what, you need to determine 'who'.

It would be a shame for you to turn up with a well-constructed purpose and speech only to find the audience doesn't understand the examples you have developed to support your theme.

1. Outstanding characteristics such as age variants, gender mix, education levels and socio-economic background.

2. Attitudes towards the subject matter.

3. How much do they know about the subject you have been asked to speak on?

4. What expectation (or lack of expectation) could this audience have of this speech?

Question Four
Why will they listen to me?

You will be able to determine the answer to this question by choosing one of the following reasons:

1. They know about this subject and will treat it like a favorite movie or book, with anticipation and endearment.

2. They have just started an initiative similar to what you are speaking about and will enjoy the experience you have in this subject.

3. The subject is one that most of this audience know very little about.

4. This subject is relevant to where their industry/company/family/ career/ marriage - is positioned right now.

You will be able to identify a reason more tailored to your audience by using one of these four 'generic' reasons and building off them.

A Fantastic Idea

I heard a story about a young man who approached Leonard Bernstein, the famous composer.

"I have a fantastic idea for a play," he exclaimed.
Bernstein said, "I'd love to hear it. Write it on the back of your business card."

The young man was incredulous, "I can't possibly put the whole idea on that small space!"

Bernstein replied, **"Then you don't have a usable concept.**

Question Five
How long do I have to speak?

Of all the questions...this is the easiest one to answer>

Imagine having a well prepared, outstanding 45 minute speech only to find out you have just twenty minutes to deliver it? If you know that you have 15 minutes... then you will know... all you need are three major points, each with a supporting example or story.

For example:

Your time schedule for a 15-minute speech would look something like the diagram below. Knowing how long you have to speak will determine how much information you will require. In some cases, you may have one story that is split into key points and then a close. You can answer each of these questions in 21 words or less and find yourself with the solid foundation you need to build an outstanding speech.

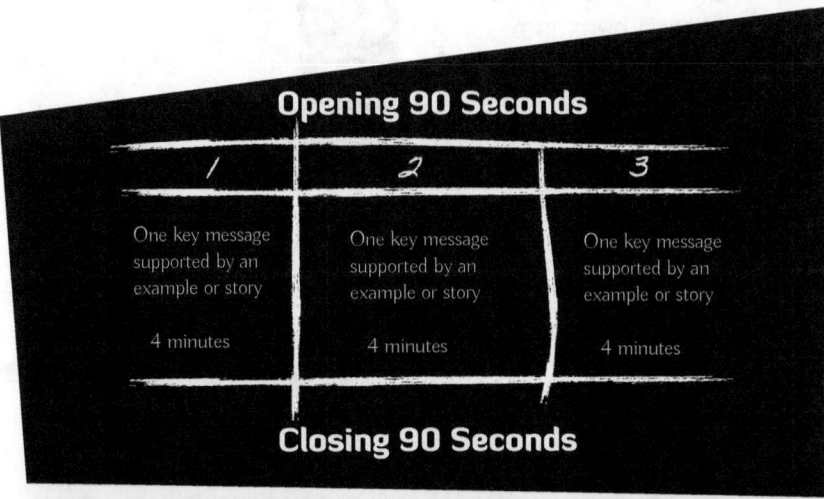

Opening 90 Seconds		
1	*2*	*3*
One key message supported by an example or story	One key message supported by an example or story	One key message supported by an example or story
4 minutes	4 minutes	4 minutes
Closing 90 Seconds		

Five Question Master Page

Why was I asked to give this speech? The reason is:

What is my topic and goal? My topic and goal is:

Who am I speaking to? The speech is for:

Why will they listen to me? They will listen because:

How long do I have to speak? My speech length is:

Developing a Speech Mindset

Before building our speech, let's note two very important principles:

Principle One ⟶ **What Before How**

This first principle relates to really knowing what you're talking about before you concentrate on how you're going to say it.

It is almost impossible to focus your mind on two dominant thoughts at one time. So, when your mind is totally focused on the 'what' of your speech it is very hard for it to pay any attention to the 'how' (delivery).

If your content is clear, and well- organized in your head and if you really understand it inside out, you can focus on your delivery.

You need to think about your main points, your ideas and your stories thoroughly. This way your content is robust, well-thought out and supported and you can do it justice in your method of presentation.

Principle Two ⟶ **Bundle Into Three**

The human brain has a real attraction to information being bundled into threes.

For example, we all grew up hearing the story of the Three Little Pigs and the Three Blind Mice. Robert O. Skovgard, editor of The Executive Speaker Newsletter writes "The most powerful and versatile speech-writing devices or techniques involve grouping of elements in units of three."

No one really knows how or why the Law of Three came to be. Were we born with it? Is it in our DNA structure?

What we do know is...when it comes to writing and delivering a powerful speech or business presentation, the Law of Three works 100% of the time, every time!

Audience research shows that most people tend to 'turn off' when they are subjected to a list of bullet-points and other listed factoids. But the prospect of just three ideas, or three steps, maybe three reasons, well, most audiences 'turn themselves back on' and listen.

Why is the bundling into three so effective?

The first item sets the basic situation, the second item shows the pattern of expectation and the third item shows completion.

For example:

You have a beginning, **1** a middle **2** and an ending. **3**

You have a way into your story **1** a way to tell your story **2** and a way to end your story. **3**

In fact, every outstanding speech will always have a title **1** a subject **2** and a purpose. **3**

As you can see, the Principle of Three works all the time and as an outstanding speaker, you will use it often.

When you use the Principle of Three, you can create a rhythm that causes a positive and pleasing sense of completion and fulfillment.

So, with these two principles in mind, let's start developing your speech.

> "When people ask me about this company I tell them three things."
>
> Steve Ballmer
> CEO, Microsoft

Headline Two

CONTENT

Build Content Around A Theme

In building your content a most effective way is to create a theme and establish it as the dominant thought...then, leverage it!

By that I mean, make it into a statement that your audience can walk away with.

For example, 'When the going gets tough, the tough get going.'

A theme is like an anchor for your audience, helping them to remember your speech. You can use your theme as an opening or a closing.

Here is an example...Opening: "Today I want to talk about the tough times that many people could be facing over the next year. My message is simple – when the going gets tough, the tough get going."

Here is another example where the theme and the opening, as well as the goal, are all wrapped into one statement: **"Thank you and good evening everyone. My goal today is to enlist your help in educating the children of our communities."**

In this example the theme is 'educating our children.' The goal is 'enlisting the help of this audience.'

To use the theme as a closing statement we can approach it from the past tense.

For example, "Today I have covered how we can educate our children in our communities and now I ask you to seriously consider helping us. Thank you for inviting me to share this evening with you."

In order for you to become a confident public speaker you will need to have a strong anchor to hold stories and ideas together.

Your theme is your anchor.

Without this anchor you will find it more difficult to establish clarity and focus - and without clarity and focus, you will never become an outstanding public speaker.

Identify Key Points

An outstanding speech has only a few key points. If you identify 10 or 12 key points you will most likely confuse or lose your audience. So we will employ the Law of Three to help us. Initially you want to work around three key points and then build out from them as you need – and as your time allows.

When you are developing your key points, use energising words or phrases which communicate confidence, purpose and action. Be aware of words or phrases that are lazy or redundant. Make sure every word works hard for you – as you really don't want to carry passengers.

For example, if the topic was 'Success' our key points could be:

1. To be successful in life and business a person needs to have a clear sense of direction.
2. Success demands commitment and concentration.
3. Passion and enthusiasm are essential for success in any endeavor.

In these three key points we now have a solid platform for building an outstanding speech. Look at the words that we can leverage off...

clear direction

commitment

concentration

endeavor

enthusiasm

life & business

Support Key Points

Every point needs to be supported. By that I mean it needs to have substance and life brought into it.

1. Stories attract the attention of an audience cause them to listen mo

The brilliant thread that brings all of your points together is the story.

2. Stories offer entertainment.

This art of story telling has been around since year dot. At the heart of storytelling, you will find the need to inform and entertain.

3. Stories provide a change pace.

In Roman times, the wealthy classes paid singers at banquets to chant, strum instruments and tell tales about their great gods, their loves, and their victories.

4. Stories teach but not preach.

5. Stories bond a speaker to an audience through a common life system - the story.

In fact, if you look closely, stories define our lives.

They bring information and context together – creating meaning and purpose.

6. Stories remind us of who we are and where we've been.

To be an interesting speaker, you will need to develop the art of finding, developing and delivering a story that is relevant to both your audience and the subject.

7. Stories enhance memorability. It makes y look good!

Stories grab the attention of the audience simply because we all have stories in our lives.

Outstanding public speakers use stories to drive their themes more than any other source of support.

The pictures that the stories create will live far longer in the mind of the audience than the actual words spoken.

Your story helps you accomplish two outcomes.

1.
Help your speech stay alive, long after your words have faded and been forgotten.

2.
Help your audience to be stimulated, at an emotional level, into your speech.

Common Story Types

Supporting stories will differ in length and shape. The following is a list that comes from Joanna Slan's book -' Using Stories & Humor - Grab Your Audience

Fables
A fable is a short story of an everyday deed told to teach a moral value using animals as characters. A great example of this is 'Who Moved My Cheese' by Spencer Johnson MD.

Anecdotes
Anecdotes are usually humorous or pointed accounts of something that has happened to someone we know or have read about. Reader's Digest, or business journals is a brilliant source of humorous, dramatic, fresh and powerful anecdotes.

Fairy Tales
A fairy tale is a short to medium length story told to entertain using supernatural characters. For example Cinderella had a fairy godmother save her from a life of never-ending drudgery by dressing her up and sending her to the ball where she met her prince and eventually lived happily ever after.

Personal Anecdotes
An anecdote is a short story drawn from everyday life, told to entertain, enlighten, and educate using human characters.

Five Essentials For Telling An Outstanding Story

For example:

~~ep your story short~~
~~simple but use enough~~
~~il to make it feel~~
~~plete.~~

"She was sitting in a rocking chair knitting socks."

This lacks significant detail so we will help it come alive.

Let's add some detail to flesh it out a little... "My grandmother was sitting in the oak rocker knitting three dark blue socks for Gumboots, our three legged, no-tailed cat."

When significant details have been added, a picture begins to form in the mind of the audience with more clarity.

Significant detail often shares quality gems about a character or make up of a person, bringing life to the story.

You could say "The man was huge" or you could say, "He was six foot three, weighed about 265 pounds and strode like a sumo wrestler."

2. Show, don't tell.

The difference between significant detail and 'show, don't tell' is in the actions you use to accompany the detail. The picture begins to form in the audience's mind and they connect more easily with the point you want to make.

By varying the gender and characters in your stories, you give the audience a chance to see themselves in the stories that you tell. If you have several characters in your story, use a voice change to show the difference. It can be a tedious time for the audience if you keep the same pattern in your delivery.

3. Plan for a varie of characters - t give you more leverage with y audien

One word of caution, you are best advised to make sure your attempt at creating a dialect will not offend others in your audience.

4. Develop a sense of action with the use of 'action' oriented words and language.

For example "Eugene moved down the hallway."

This is a weak pattern to employ in telling the story. It can be made more dynamic by saying it this way: "Eugene inched slowly down the narrow dark hallway."

The 'inched slowly' inclusion begins to create a sense of tension and by linking it to 'narrow dark hallway' it builds mystery.

For example, you could be telling the story about a school teacher who helped you years ago, and slant it towards a number of different things depending on your speech:

5. Find a good slant

- Her dedication
- Her ability to make subjects come alive
- Her ability to inspire boundless possibilities for each of her students.

Find ways to make a comparison between things that are different.

For example, Shakespeare did this well when he compared a hand with the texture and color of a bird's feather. In 'The Winter's Tale', he writes, "As soft as a dove's down and as white."

Another example is found in a speech delivered by Eugene A. Ludwig in Los Angeles, July 24 1995, commenting on Federal Regulatory Reform.

He said, "Being a regulator these days is a lot like being the nearest fire hydrant to the dog pound. You know they'll have to turn to you in an emergency – but its sure tough dealing with those daily indignities."

Look for stories that can drive a critical point you want to make.

Here is a story by Dr Norman Vincent Peale that I have used often to support a key point.

Dr Norman Vincent Peale was walking through the streets of Kowloon and he came to a tattoo studio. He saw one that said 'Born To Lose' and asked the tattoo artist if anyone ever bought that one. The tattoo man told Dr Peale, "Many times." Dr Peale asked why someone would put that on their body and the tattoo man said in broken English, "Before tattooed on body – tattooed in mind."

In the tattoo story there are two subjects I expand on to establish a connection between the theme and the audience:

- **Why would someone want to tattoo 'Born To Lose' on their body?**
- **Can this attitude exist in business?**

This story has been used as a supporting point in a conference speech I deliver called **'Winning is an Inside Job'**.

Using a story for validation
Validation brings a fact, statistic or some 'source of proof' into the equation. In the tattoo story, the validation could be demographics of the number of business professionals that have sabotaged their success with negative mind-sets. In fact, you could use an increasing statistic, moving from local to regional, to national, to international statistics that show the growth of tattooing.

Using the story as your foundation
I recommend you use a story, or stories, as the foundation for all of your speaking opportunities. It makes a clear point, pulls together your speech, entertains your audience and makes it memorable all at once!

Keeping The Attention Of Your Audience

When making your speech, you will need to understand the relationship between the attention capability of your audience and the amount of time that you are speaking.

A speech starts out with a hopeful audience. They hope the speaker will be good.

Their attention is moderately high at the beginning but left on their own, and without any help from the speaker, they will slowly lose attention until the magic words "In Conclusion" are spoken.

The graph below demonstrates this.

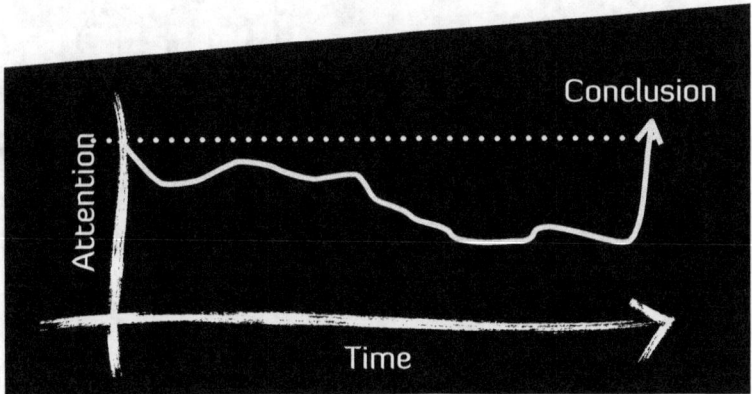

So the question is how does a speaker keep the attention of the audience above the halfway mark for the whole speech? The answer is, you use **'Speech Hooks'**. You can use them every 2-3 minutes to **hook the attention of your audience back** to where you want them.

Below is a list of the most common speech hooks. **Please note**, a speech hook is not limited to this list. Use your imagination and develop your own library of attention grabbers.

visual aid
visual aid

questions
questions

video
video

stories
stories

illustrations
illustrations

planned movement
planned movement

demonstrations
demonstrations

eye contact
eye contact

hand gestures
hand gestures

humor
humor

Using Humor

You will find humor everywhere you look. Even the most serious person has a sense of humor buried somewhere in their personality.

People in your audience have been raised in the MTV environment and they expect to see and hear more than a dying speaker who is bludgeoning them to death with a boring delivery style.

There are three important questions to ask as you approach making humor part of your speech.

1. When do I need to use humor?
2. How much do I need to use?
3. How do I make it relevant to my point?

If you cannot answer these three questions perhaps you might be best not using too much humor in your speech.

Types of Humor

Humor, as a speech hook, is becoming an important ingredient in speeches, much to the pleasure of audiences. So let's look at some of the most common forms of humor used in a speech.

The Joke
Made up funny story that most o_en involves the challenge of a stereotype or common event. A joke seldom has a point of its own and this allows you to easily connect it to your speech point, provided it is relevant.

The One-Liner
A funny saying, quote or comment. These may be used to emphasize a point or to connect one point to another.

The Punch Word
A word that becomes critical to the sentence or point being funny.

The Punch Phrase
A phrase or sentence that turns a subject in a different direction and creates clever humor.

For example, "Last Christmas was a stressful time for me. My poor family were often at the receiving end of my stress, so I was surprised on Christmas day to open my present from my wife to find a 12-month membership to a relaxation health club with spa. I said "This is so fantastic and must have cost you a lot." My wife replied, "Not really. A lot of people chipped in."

The punch phrase is **'a lot of people chipped in'** and this phrase brings the story to life by creating a new slant as well as a humorous conclusion.

The Foundation

Provides background to a joke or punch phrase. The foundation for my Christmas present story was how I had become grouchy and difficult to live with in recent months.

The Layer

This is when you build the story with several 'interactions', like punch phrases or words, or short anecdotes.

The Flashback

When you repeat a word or phrase in your speech to remind your audience about a funny segment of your speech that you have already delivered.

Cartoon design by Sean d'Souza www.psychotactics.com

Headline Three

13 BOX STRUCTURE

The 13 Box Structure System

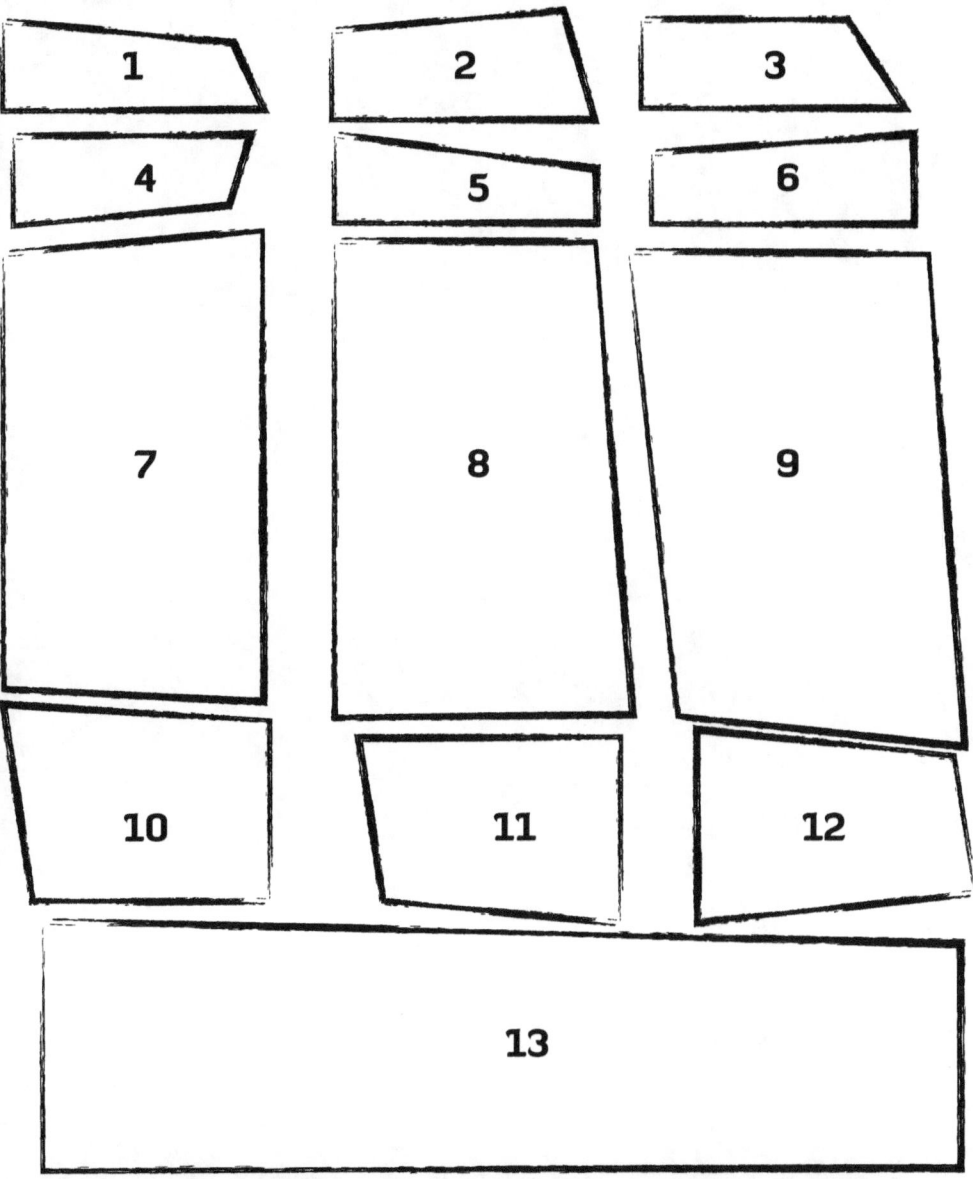

To talk about your business effectively, you will need a way of organizing your thoughts, ideas, and value propositions, as well as other important business messages.

Knowing how to organize your thoughts in such a way that they are easy to talk about and for your audience to follow is fundamental to becoming a memorable, outstanding business communicator.

eryone
us have a
uirement to talk
out our business.
ne of us can escape

e only question now
are we good at it?

That's where the 13 Box Structure System comes in.

This System has been proven to work in hundreds of business presentations, conferences, in-house meetings, negotiations, public speeches - just to name a few, and is perhaps one of the most an effective and easy-to-use methods for organising and delivering your important business information.

The 13 Box Structure System

Before I give you the step by step process for writing and delivering a 13 Box Presentation, let me share **three little secrets** about making this System really work like a charm for you.

Always follow the numbers, both in writing and delivering. Trying to take a shortcut can often result in your communication missing the bulls-eye.

Always follow the numbers!

Write in bullet points.

Write using bullet-points so you don't end up reading. (With a bullet point you can talk about the subject.

This allows you to have a more natural, conversational voice which is more inviting and memorable.)

Practice from the structure chart. (By using this chart to write your presentation, and then practicing it, talking about the bullet points, you begin to take complete ownership. Doing this two or three will help to imprint your presentation into your mind.)

Practice from the 13 B structure chart.

Okay, now let's get started.

The Five Steps Of Writing

Just as there are disciplined steps in delivering the 13 Box Presentation, there are discipline steps to writing. **The sequence of writing is just as important as the sequence of delivery.** By following the numbers you begin to layer the information in your mind, helping you to retain and use effectively.

Step One: Write The Conclusion.

The first step in writing your presentation is to start with the conclusion.!

You will need to ask yourself **three questions** in when you write your closing statement:

1. What action do you want your audience to take?

Do you want them to either start or stop doing something, or do you want them to change to or from something?

Do you want them to feel or experience something?

This action is either physical, emotional or logical. Whichever one ever it is, write it down in 21 words or less.

2. Why should your audience take this action?

This is not about you, it is about them. What is the 'valued outcome' that your audience will receive when to take the action you want them to? Once again, write it down in 21 words or less.

3. **How** can this audience take the action you want them to?

This is the where the rubber meets the road. How does this audience take action? Do they follow a system you've designed, or do they sign a document? Once again write your answer in 21 words or less.

Now that you have all three answers, shape them into **one closing statement that communicates what action you want your audience to take,** why they should take it and how they can act on it.

Step 1	Action Conclusion Statement What? Why? How?	Box 13

Step Two: Headline Titles

This is a critical step in keeping your content organized. You can shape your Headlines into a number of sequences. The key to helping your audience stay with you throughout the presentation is found in keeping them clearly informed, always, on where you are at any given point, and where you will be taking them next in this presentation.

In essence, when you use Headline Titles you create a critical path that allows your audience to stay with you at all times.

There are four basic Key Subject Headline patterns:

equential

Sequential is a natural flowing pattern. that presents events as they occur, e.g., the steps necessary to start a new business or install a new system into the business. A Chronological Sequence goes further and provides a specific time context to the events.

The Topical pattern is useful for when the presentation lacks any clear pattern, or the presentation isn't confined to a procedure, process, or time. You assign meaningful labels to subtopics, which are all related to the Action Conclusion.

2. Topical

For example, if your Action Conclusion was 'Approve our budget increase request so we can complete the project, enabling our sales team to increase sales performance and achieve the growth mandate', The Topical pattern could be:

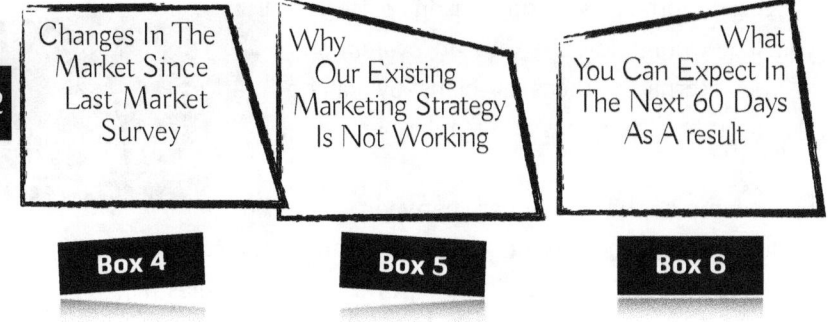

tep 2

Changes In The Market Since Last Market Survey	Why Our Existing Marketing Strategy Is Not Working	What You Can Expect In The Next 60 Days As A result
Box 4	**Box 5**	**Box 6**

The Problem & Solution pattern is commonly used in technical presentations but can still be effective for any presentation where you need to show **'what is, what ought to be** and **what needs to be done.'**

3.
Problem &
Solution

Often this pattern will include: **Symptoms of the problem.** This is where you will focus on helping the audience recognise that there is a problem and that it needs to be solved. **Possible solutions.**

Any presentation that addresses a problem, of any complexity, will not only list solutions but also include constraints on the solutions, an overall evaluation of them, a recommendation of the best solution or combination of solutions.

You can use the problem & solution pattern most effectively when you want the audience to make a decision and take an action.

In the Contrast & Comparison pattern you lead your audience into an evaluation of the alternative ideas or plans by calling attention to differences and similarities.

4.
Contrast &
Comparison

For example, the difference between a 'closed mind and an open mind,' or 'contracting versus hiring employees', or 'the different ways two companies face a crisis'.

All these examples use Contrast and Comparison not only to illustrate but also to provide structure to the presentation.

Third Step: Critical Message Summary

One of the best ways to shape a Critical Message Summary is to ask this question: **'If I could only make three statements about this Headline, what would they be?'**

Imagine a target and in the center is a bull's-eye. The bull's-eye represents the absolute must have information. This is the information the audience **MUST HAVE** if they are going to be able to take the action you want them to take.

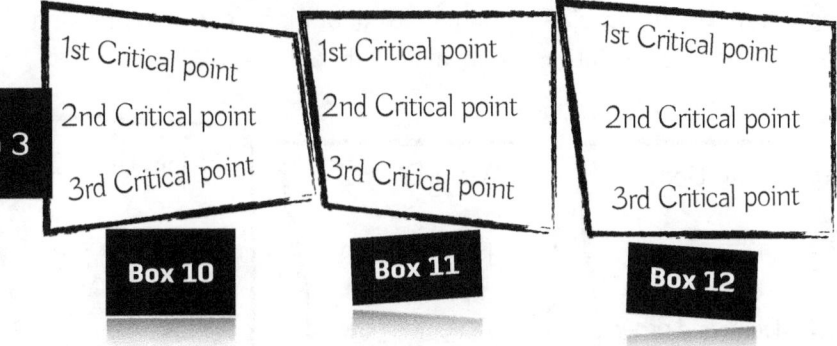

An effective Critical Message Summary can have less than three **but not more** than three .

The power of the critical message is in identifying **the absolutely essential information** that has to be presented if you are to achieve your Action Conclusion.

Your audience cannot make their decision without this information.

Step Four: The Main Bodies

The fourth step in the writing process is to begin shaping the three Main Bodies, which expands on the Critical Messages providing detail and depth by expanding clarifying, illustrating, substantiating and demonstrating.

While you will have three Critical Messages, your Main body may have up to seven points that you need to present if you are to achieve success. The Main Body will present testimonies from appropriate sources, clarify points with quotations, explanations, and anecdotes or by restating the ideas in different ways.

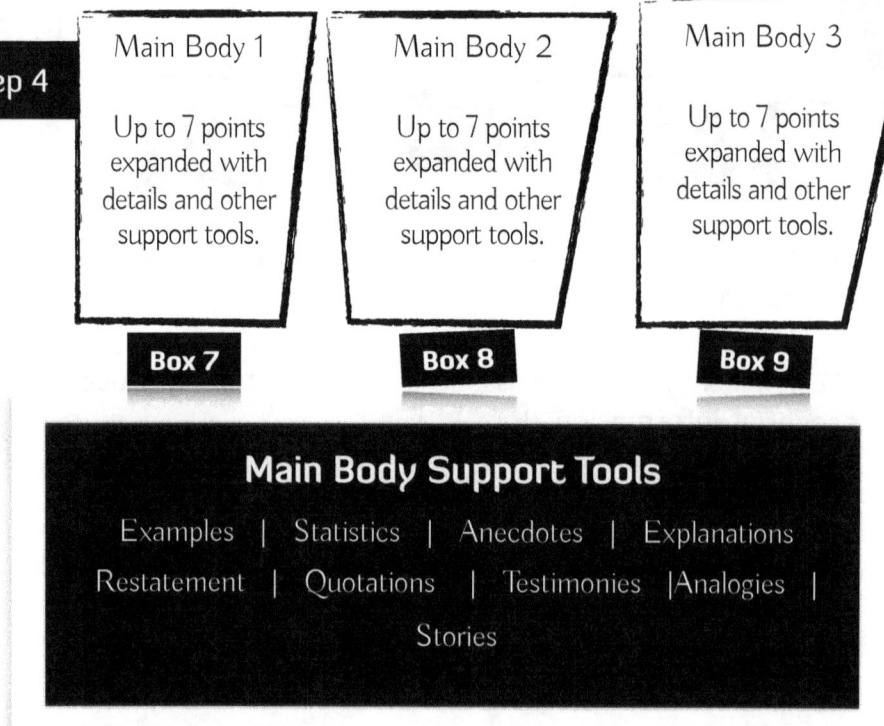

Step 4

Main Body 1

Up to 7 points expanded with details and other support tools.

Box 7

Main Body 2

Up to 7 points expanded with details and other support tools.

Box 8

Main Body 3

Up to 7 points expanded with details and other support tools.

Box 9

Main Body Support Tools

Examples | Statistics | Anecdotes | Explanations

Restatement | Quotations | Testimonies |Analogies |

Stories

Step Five: The Opening Sequence

This involves three steps:

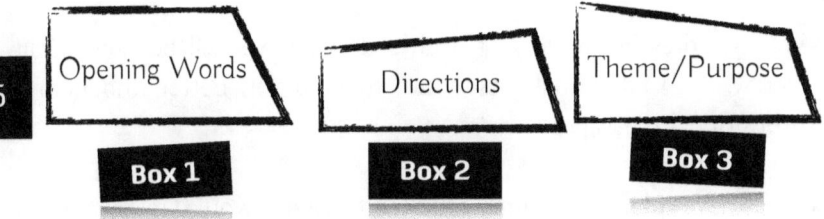

Step 1 is the Opening Words. With the right opening words you can engage any audience, of any size.

You can use a questions, a dramatic statement, a quote, a statistic or a simple positioning statement, like this: **"Thank you Roger. Good afternoon everyone. We want to thank you for the invitation to meet with you today. It has been an exciting year and now that we have entered into the final quarter we have reached an interesting and challenging crossroad."**

The **opening words help settle the nerves or tensions** that may be resident in both you and your audience. The opening words also lead directly into the second step, which is -

Step Two: Provide Clear Direction.

This is where you let your audience know:How long you will be speaking and What they can do while you are presenting to them. (Do they take notes or will they get a handout? How about questions? When do they ask them?)

For example:

- Today we will be presenting for about 25 minutes and then we will open up for a discussion. We've prepared a set of notes for you, as you can see.

- These notes are a copy of each slide that we will be presenting today, with additional foot notes, to help you better understand our critical messages.

- We have plenty of time today, so if you would rather ask a question as we progress, feel free to do so, otherwise we can wait and answer them when we have finished.

Step 3 is the Theme or Purpose:

This final step in the Opening Sequence **positions the presentation with purpose** by letting the audience know why it is taking place. This sends a powerful message to your audience that that you are in control and have very clear, and definite path you want to lead them down.

When you write your Opening Sequence following this model you find yourself instilling confidence in your audience - because it let's them know that you know what you are doing. **They are safe in your hands.**

Well, now that we've written the presentation, it's time to deliver it.

Delivering The 13 Box Speech

Once you have followed the five steps of writing your speech, it's time to 'Stand & Deliver'. This is where the real magic of the 13 Box Structure System comes into it's own.

Delivering your presentation becomes deceptively easy because now all you need to do is **FOLLOW THE NUMBERS!**

That's right - all the hard works has been done in the writing phase. Just to show you how easy it is, **let me give you an example**. Imagine I am standing in front of a small group of decision-makers who will be deciding on whether or not we need more funding for a critical project. I'll use the Opening Sequence, transitioning into the three Headlines.

Box 1: Opening Words:

"Thank you Roger. Good afternoon everyone. We want to thank you for the invitation to meet with you today. It has been an exciting year and now that we have entered into the final quarter we have reached an interesting and challenging crossroad.

Box 2: Directions

Today we will be talking for about 25 minutes and then we will open up for a discussion. We've prepared a set of notes for you, as you can see. These notes are a copy of each slide that we will be presenting today, with additional foot notes, to help you better understand our critical messages.

We do have plenty of time today, so if you would rather ask a question as we progress, feel free to do so, otherwise we can wait and answer them when we have finished.

Box 3: Theme / Purpose:

The purpose of our presentation today is to seek the approval of a budget increase so we can complete the project, enabling our sales team to increase sales performance and achieve the growth mandate.

Transition into Headline Sequence:

So, today, we will be covering three key areas:

Headline 1: First I will talk about the Changes in the market since our last market survey.

Headline 2: Then Sarah will talk about Why our Existing Marketing Plan Is Not Working and ...

Headline 3: I will come back and outline What You Can Expect In 60 Days as a Result of approving our request today, and...then we'll close and answer any questions."

From this point you move into your Main Body 1. Just as easy as 1-2-3 you are into your presentation. **Can you see the delivery pattern? The golden rule is to follow the numbers. Stay horizontal before going vertical.**

Now let's look at your presentation as it will be presented using the 13 Box Structure System.

13 Box Structure Chart Model

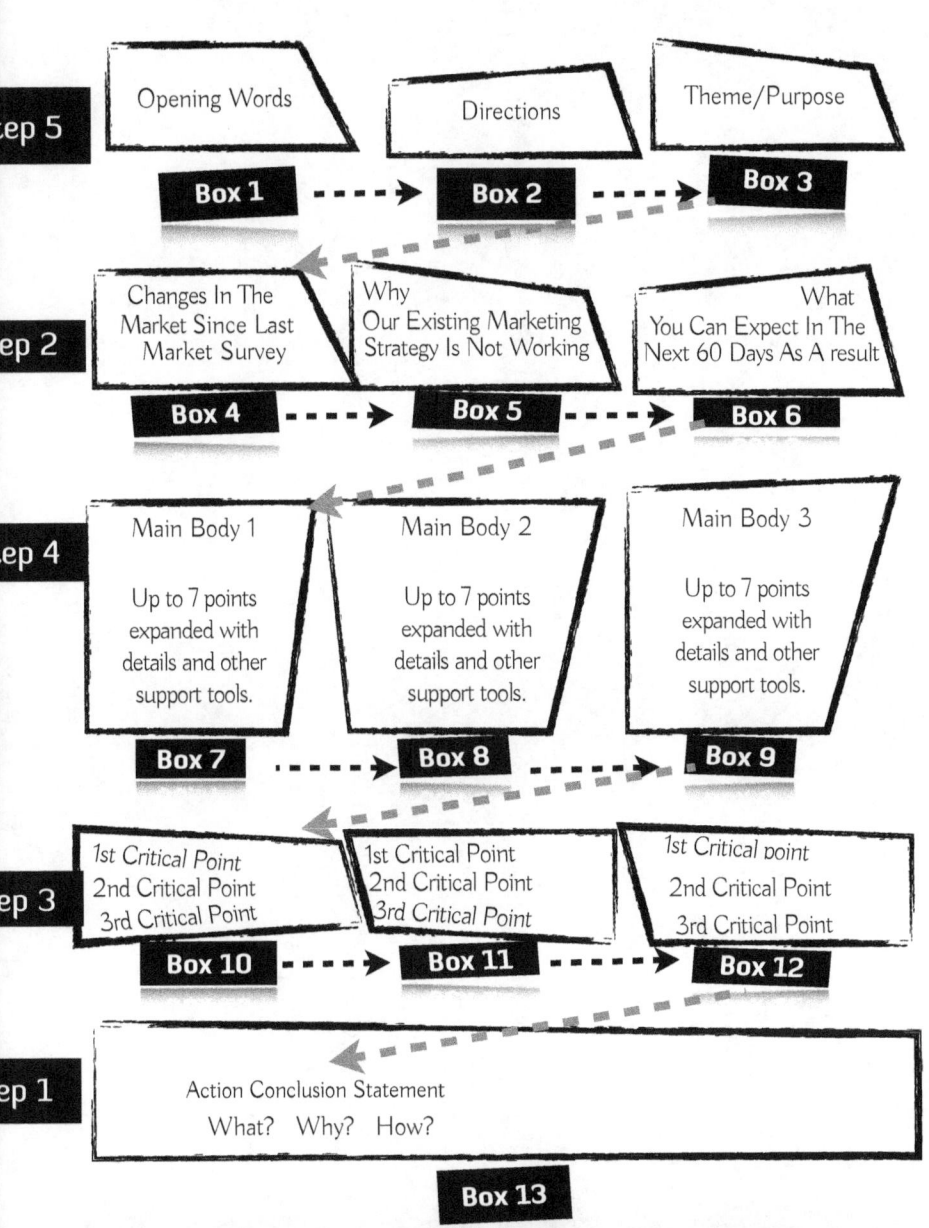

The Final Words

Now that we have finished this little book the question is, "What have you learned?"

You have not learned rules and regulations. Instead you have learned questions to ask and answer, steps to follow and disciplines to adhere to.

Ultimately you have learned to be yourself and tell your stories and be interesting.

Don't try to be another speaker, be you!

Be authentic, your audience will love you for it and you will be asked to come back and speak again. Why? Because you are on your way to becoming an outstanding public speaker and we all know, people love to be in an audience when an outstanding public speaker is in control.

By following the guidelines in this book, you will prepare and deliver powerful business speeches. These techniques and tools are 'tried and tested'. They are safe, and using them will not embarrass you. In fact, you will notice an immediate lift in your confidence and your audience will come up to you and thank you for a well-delivered, easy-to-understand speech.

There is no mystery to developing a great speech, only simple steps to follow and now you have them.

I wish you outstanding success in your speaking endeavors. Write me and let me know all about your victories.

Eugene

A little about me...

I have over 22 years experience in working with executive level management in the niche area of business presentations and proposals. My core business is helping business people talk about their business better. The tools I use for this is Training, Coaching and Consulting.

Over the past 22 years I've has been an Emcee, Key Note Speaker, Strategy Facilitator, Transition Catalyst, Trusted Advisor, Workshop Designer and Facilitator, Proposal Writer and Pitch Strategist, Coach and Mentor to executive level management.

What I brings to a business relationship is experience, knowledge and wisdom. The combination of these three always mean a profitable outcome at the end of the day.

Including this one, I've written two books: The Public Speakers Little Black Book and Dare To Dream Again (both available from my website www.moreaucommunications.com) and I am creator of the 13 Box Structure System for business presentations and the Find, Win, Keep & Grow methodology for business strategy.

I am a Certified Master Coach (CMC) from the Behavioural Coaching Institute in Australia and I've personally trained or coached numerous 'C' level management in presentation skills, relationship management, high level proposal skills and internal communication strategies in New Zealand, Australia, Singapore, Bahrain, Japan, UK and USA.

I am an experienced stage presenter and have addressed conferences in New Zealand, Australia, Jakarta and the USA as a Key Note Speaker and Workshop Leader on a variety of leadership, communication and relationship topics and people have often described me as a burst of energy on the audience.

If you would like to read more about what people have to say me and the work I've done with them please visit my website.

What People Are Saying...

"In my wildest dreams I'd have never imagined a single book to be so useful to my business. You see when I first ran into Eugene's little black book at a seminar, I was just attending yet another seminar. I had no idea that this book would change everything I did. I had no idea that it would make me so relaxed at speaking. Not a clue that it would help me drive home my message with greater impact than ever before.

This little book isn't a little book. It's a book that will take over your life. It will change how you do your presentations. It will change the structure of your presentations. It will change the results you've been getting so far. It will, in short - take over your life.

Every presentation we do, every speech we give, every interview we conduct is built on the rock-solid structure that you'll find within this book. I wish more speakers had this book. It would keep me awake at more seminars!"

Sean D'Souza | www.psychotactics.com

"I have known Eugene for many years. He is a truly inspirational speaker and trainer, with a genuine heart to help others become more powerful and engaging communicators. This easy- to-read little book represents some 30 years of distilled wisdom by one of the best."

Dick Brunton | Executive Chair | Colmar Brunton

"It's not only the fear of public speaking but the fear of being asked to speak that constantly haunts many of us. Eugene, clearly, simply and comprehensively covers this subject better than anyone. This book will be an international best seller! I would recommend this book to first time speakers right through to experienced speakers. A must for every manager, businessperson and anyone involved in sales."

Jim Hainey | Managing Director | Speakers New Zealand

"The Public Speaker's Little Black Book taught me more about this subject than four years of attending weekly Toastmasters meetings."
Trevor Johnston | Business Coach and Entrepreneur

"Eugene Moreau's Public Speaker's Little Black Book is the only book you need on this subject. Eugene is a world class communicator and this book is a world class book on communicating to a group. This book actually makes me want to give speeches!"
Philippa Weaver | Founder | www.greensky.co.nz

"While so called 'experts' in the public speaking field abound it is very rare that they are able to pass on their expertise and knowledge to others. Eugene's 'Little Black Book' is informative, sensible, practical, concise, easy to follow and implement. It will help those who struggle in this area, as well as those who are looking to improve and develop their skills. I will certainly be using it every time I am faced with having to speak and will be recommending that my colleagues and friends get their hands on a copy as soon as possible!"
Meg Tillet | Sysmex New Zealand Limited

"Eugene is a passionate communicator and his passion for helping others improve their skills is particularly evident in this book. I use the foundations he has laid out here every time I am asked to speak and it has given me the resource to plan and structure any speech for any occasion with confidence."
Stuart Cairns | Investment Banker

his little book isn't a little book.

's a book that will take over your life. It will
hange how you do your presentations.

will change the structure of your
resentations.

will change the results you've been getting so
ar. It will, in short - take over your life.

very presentation we do, every speech we
ive, every interview we conduct is built on the
ock-solid structure that you'll find within this
ook. I wish more speakers had this book. It
ould keep me awake at more seminars!"

ean D'Souza www.psychotactics.com

ISBN 978-1-4466-1545-4
90000
9 781446 615454

The Public Speaker's Little Black Book

Eugene Moreau

THE PUBLIC SPEAKER'S
LITTLE BLACK BOOK

How To Be An Outstanding Speaker Demystified.

By Eugene Moreau

This little book isn't a little book.

It's a book that will take over your life. It will change how you do your presentations.

It will change the structure of your presentations.

It will change the results you've been getting so far. It will, in short - take over your life.

Every presentation we do, every speech we give, every interview we conduct is built on the rock-solid structure that you'll find within this book. I wish more speakers had this book. It would keep me awake at more seminars!"

Sean D'Souza www.psychotactics.com

ISBN 978-1-4466-1545-4

THE PUBLIC SPEAKER'S
LITTLE BLACK BOOK

How To Be An Outstanding Speaker Demystified.

By Eugene Moreau

The Public Speaker's Little Black Book

Eugene Moreau

www.ingramcontent.com/pod-product-compliance
Lightning Source LLC
Chambersburg PA
CBHW051236170526
45165CB00004B/1455